S0-BOA-566

THINK BIGGER!

MORE SPECIAL PROJECTS FOR CREATIVE THINKING

BIG AL

WRITTEN BY MARTHA SYMONDS • ILLUSTRATED BY BEV ARMSTRONG

The
Learning
Works

Copyright © 1993 by The Learning Works, Inc.

All rights reserved.

The purchase of this book entitles the individual teacher to reproduce copies for use in the classroom. The reproduction of any part of this book for an entire school or school system or for commercial use is strictly prohibited.

Other than as described above, no part of this book may be reproduced or utilized in any form or by any means, electronic or mechanical—including photocopying and recording—or by any information or retrieval system, without written permission from the publisher. Inquiries should be addressed to the Permissions Department,

The Learning Works, Inc.
P.O. Box 6187
Santa Barbara, California 93160

ISBN: 0-88160-260-4
LW 255

Printed in the United States of America.
Current Printing (last digit): 10 9 8 7 6 5 4 3 2

Introduction

THINK BIGGER! is designed to provide opportunities for the development of cognitive skills. These learning activities help encourage creative thinking and the expression of unique approaches and solutions to specific tasks and problems. **THINK BIGGER!** is a book to get kids thinking!

Cognitive skills such as applying, synthesizing, inferring, comprehending, predicting, asking important questions, classifying, analyzing, knowledge retention, and evaluating are emphasized in **THINK BIGGER!**

The activities in **THINK BIGGER!** may by used by individual students or by small or large groups in classroom learning centers. They may also be used as homework assignments. The projects include specific directions for students; they require little or no teacher direction.

In evaluating a student's work, teachers may wish to look for the following as evidence of growth in cognitive skills:

- ability to remember main ideas and details
- ability to present an idea or point of view and explain it
- ability to create novel and imaginative designs
- ability to generate and write unique solutions to problems
- ability to classify, categorize, and explain
- ability to apply previously acquired knowledge to new problems or situations
- ability to compare or contrast similar elements in different situations
- ability to predict outcomes imaginatively and logically
- ability to identify relevant material and to ask relevant questions
- ability to evaluate situations, and to present arguments and well-reasoned points of view

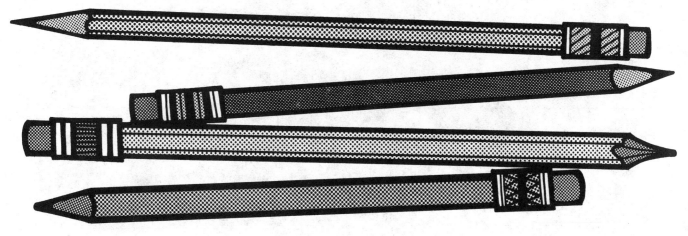

3

Contents

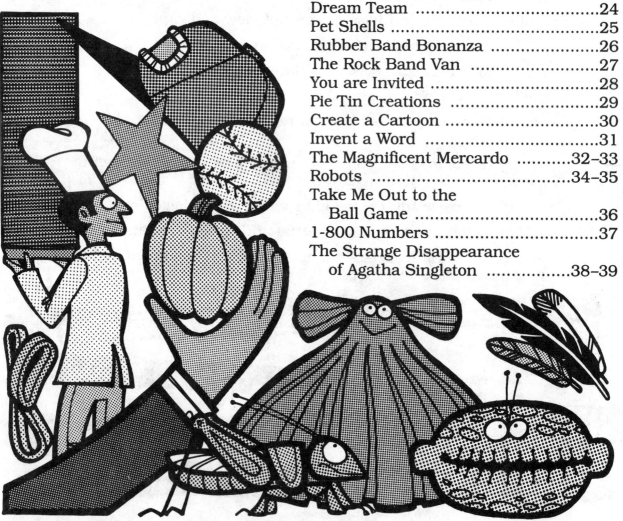

Contents

Think Bigger!
© 1993—The Learning Works, Inc.

Messy Martin

Messy Martin can't find anything when he needs it. He wants a practical piece of furniture where he can neatly store all of the following:

- 12 pairs of socks
- a TV and a VCR
- 10 pairs of shoes
- 4 pairs of jeans
- a baseball card collection

- 4 photo albums
- 30 paperback books
- 6 baseball caps
- 10 T-shirts
- miscellaneous sports equipment

Think about how to help Martin organize. On a separate piece of paper, design a useful piece of furniture for him that includes shelves, drawers, cabinets, and closet space. Label each section to show where all of Martin's possessions will go.

New Titles, New Tales

"*Goldilocks and the Three Bears*," Mr. Moseby muttered. "I read the same fairy tales over and over to my fourteen grandchildren every time they come to visit. I think I'll surprise them. I'll rename one of the stories and create a new tale." So Mr. Moseby wrote a new fairy tale called *Goldie Fox and the Three Pears*. It was a story about the adventures of a woman who ran a fruit stand. Her gift of three pears to a homeless person sparked a series of wondrous surprises.

Although we never tire of the original fairy tales, it is fun to experiment with new versions. Revise the title of one of the fairy tales below. Then, on a separate piece of paper, write and illustrate a story to go with your new title.

Thumbelina	*Cinderella*
Little Red Riding Hood	*Jack and the Beanstalk*
Sleeping Beauty	*Rumplestiltskin*
The Three Little Pigs	*Hansel and Gretel*
The Three Billy Goats Gruff	*Snow White and Rose Red*

7

The Happy Hound Holiday Hotel

Many people worry about leaving their dogs behind when they go on vacation. Imagine you have found the perfect place for a family to leave their dog while they are away—The Happy Hound Holiday Hotel—a special luxury resort for dogs. The hotel owners have asked you to design a colorful brochure highlighting the unusual features of their hotel. On a separate piece of paper, design a brochure. Describe and illustrate the following:

- the dogs' rooms
- food served at the hotel
- games and activities

- equipment and toys
- grooming services
- special luxuries

Use your imagination. Nothing is too extravagant for these pampered pets.

Lost and Found

"I can't find my stuffed white lamb," Karen said tearfully to her dad as she was preparing to go to bed. "Grandma brought it all the way from New Zealand, and I can't go to sleep without it." Karen decided to ask her eight brothers and sisters if they knew where her lamb might be. These are their replies:

Kurt: The lamb was in the backyard getting all muddy from the rain. I thought it was Ken's, so I put it in his bedroom.

Kerry: Kap was playing with it outside his doghouse. I put the lamb behind the sofa so he wouldn't find it.

Kim: I found the lamb on the bookcase. It was so dirty that I put it into the laundry basket.

Karl: I saw your lamb under the dining room table. I thought it was one of Kap's toys, so I took it outside to his doghouse.

Ken: I found the lamb in my backpack when I was getting ready for school. I was in a hurry, so I laid it on top of the dishwasher.

Kyle: I saw the lamb behind the sofa when I was vacuuming. I set it on the bookcase.

Kelly: When I saw your lamb, it was on top of the dishwasher. I took it off and put it under the dining room table where I thought you would be sure to see it.

Krista: I found the lamb on the floor in Ken's bedroom. I thought it was his, so I put it in his backpack.

After listening to each person in her family, Karen knew where to look for her lamb. Where did she find it?

9

Think Bigger!
© 1993—The Learning Works, Inc.

Design a Menu

When planning a menu for a party, it is important to consider foods that go well together, the people you are entertaining, and ways to make the food attractive. Pick one of the following situations. Decide what you will serve to eat and drink. On a separate piece of paper, design a menu for the occasion.

- Ted Deems, the captain of the local football team, is coming for breakfast before the Big Game.

- A twelve-year-old girl, Wendy Todd, will serve lunch to ten of her friends on her birthday.

- The circus has come to town, and you have invited the clowns, acrobats, animal trainers, and other performers to your house for Sunday dinner.

- You and twenty-three members of your family are planning a family reunion and hike in Trilby Forest. You want to have a picnic lunch in the woods. Since fires are not permitted in Trilby Forest, everything you bring must already be cooked.

- Four members of the *Snake Eyes* rock group are coming to your house for a late-night supper after their concert.

The Miniature Golf Course

Pretend you are the designer of a nine-hole miniature golf course. Select a theme for your golf course, such as "Fantasy Fun," "Safari Golf," or "Land of Adventure."

Draw a plan for the course on a separate piece of paper. Show the layout and design of each of the holes. Use your imagination to create challenges for the players such as sand traps, ponds, streams, trees, tunnels, bridges, and other obstacles.

Think Bigger!
© 1993—The Learning Works, Inc.

Secret Codes

Andy and his brother Max love to create codes so they can write secret messages. One of their clever codes uses shapes and dots for letters of the alphabet. It looks like this:

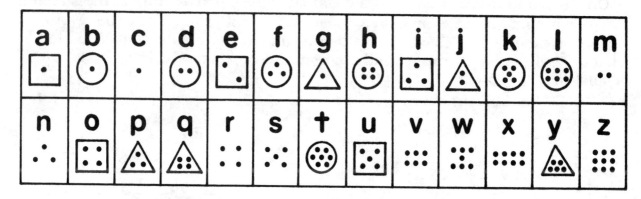

Look at the vowels in this code. What shape are they? Study the consonants in the code. What other patterns of shapes and dots were used for the consonants?

Here is a message in the shape-and-dot code that Max wrote to Andy:

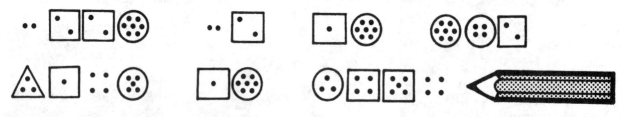

Write Max's message here.

In the space provided below, create a code of your own. You may use any symbols you choose—letters, colors, numbers, shapes, dots, or words. Share your code with a partner. Use your code to write a brief secret message. Ask a friend to decode your message.

a	b	c	d	e	f	g	h	i	j	k	l	m

n	o	p	q	r	s	t	u	v	w	x	y	z

Think Bigger!

Play Ball!

The people of Parker City have voted to build a new baseball stadium for the Parker City Giants. You have been asked to design this new stadium.

On a separate piece of paper, draw and label the different parts of the stadium. Include the following:

- baseball diamond and field
- food stands
- scoreboard
- dressing rooms for players
- warm-up area
- press box for newspaper reporters and media announcers
- spectators' seating areas
- a way for people in wheelchairs to get around the stadium

Think Bigger!
© 1993—The Learning Works, Inc.

Shopping Surprises

"Order our catalog and enjoy the convenience of shopping by mail," the Sunrise Supply Company ad said. "We are an old-fashioned general store that sells everything—food, clothing, furniture, garden supplies, toys, machines, tools, and video equipment. You name it—we have it!"

Delighted at the thought of avoiding shopping malls, Ms. Alexander opened her catalog. However, when she saw what was inside, she was distressed. "How can I possibly know what these products are? There are no descriptions, just strange-sounding names!" she exclaimed. "Is *Soft 'n White* a pillow, a stuffed rabbit, or a package of marshmallows?"

The names of other products in the Sunrise Supply Company catalog are listed on the next page. In each box, write what you think these items are. Try to think of at least two possibilities for each product name.

Shopping Surprises
(continued)

Frost Bites	Sand Man
_____ _____	_____ _____
Sock-It-to-Em	Compu-Talk
_____ _____	_____ _____
Electro-Spark	Speedmaster
_____ _____	_____ _____
Mighty Bar	Choc-o-Chunk
_____ _____	_____ _____
Whispies	Flex-a-Matic
_____ _____	_____ _____

Select one of the products above. On a separate piece of paper, write a description of it for the Sunrise Supply Company catalog. Use no more than fifty words in your description.

Think Bigger!
 © 1993—The Learning Works, Inc.

Great Shapes

"Look at these unusual animals!" David exclaimed, as he and his friend Shelly paused before the *Great Shapes* collection at the Museum of Modern Art. Every painting or sculpture in the collection was derived from a basic geometric shape like one of the following:

Some of the animals in the collection looked like this:

On a separate piece of paper, draw an imaginary animal using basic geometric shapes. Color your animal with crayons, charcoal, colored pencils, or felt-tipped pens.

The Old Foghorns

For hundreds of years, foghorns have helped ships at sea. The foghorns sound two notes—a low note and a very low note. They make this sound repeatedly. Foghorns are usually placed on rocky shores, at the entrances to harbors, on lighthouses, or on buoys. When the fog is so thick that the ship captains cannot see the shoreline or rocks in the harbor, the sound of the foghorn warns them of the danger nearby.

Last year the city of San Domingo decided to sell nine of its old foghorns and replace them with new ones. A homeowner bought one to use as a burglar alarm. A farmer bought one to call his cows to the barn. A school principal bought one to replace the dismissal bell.

On a separate piece of paper, tell who bought the other six foghorns. Describe how they plan to use them.

Think Bigger!
© 1993—The Learning Works, Inc.

No Cars Allowed

The citizens of the town of Evergreen are committed to creating a clean-air environment for their city. Part of their environmental plan involves the use of vehicles that do not burn gasoline. You have just been hired by the Clean and Green Transportation Department of the city of Evergreen to design a new vehicle for transporting people and goods.

Show your design in the space below. Label its primary parts and provide a brief explanation of how it works and how it runs without gasoline.

_____

_____

_____

_____

_____

_____

License Plate Puzzlers

Whenever Josh and his grandfather take a trip, they play a game called License Plate Puzzlers. Josh reads the license plates of the cars they pass. As soon as he spots an intriguing plate, he says its letters and numbers and tries to guess what they mean. For example:

$$\boxed{\textbf{T42}}$$

Guesses: a husband and wife who play a lot of golf—tee for two

a woman named Tracy, 42 years old

a woman who owns a company that makes tea bags—tea for two

a man named T. Fortoo

Play License Plate Puzzlers by reading the license plates below. Guess to whom they might belong by thinking about what the numbers and letters could mean. Try to find at least two meanings for each license plate. Write your responses on a separate piece of paper. Next time you travel, try playing License Plate Puzzlers with your family or friends.

HAY FEVER	RDT MFT	SPEEDY	4 BOYS
WINGS	SILVER	TUNE 4 U	SAILING
1OUSNE1	TIGERS	BAKER	BINGO

Think Bigger!
© 1993—The Learning Works, Inc.

We're Getting a Ponko

"I got a letter from Uncle Fred today, and he said he's sending us a ponko," Mrs. Banks announced to her family at dinner.

"A ponko?" Mr. Banks looked perplexed. "What is that?"

"I'm sorry, but I don't know either," his wife replied. "I couldn't find the word *ponko* in the dictionary."

"Sounds like a rare tropical bird," offered Laura Banks.

"No, I think it's a reptile," said her brother Louis, smiling mischievously.

Larry Banks, age twelve, loved computer games. "Maybe it's an electronic game that Uncle Fred has invented!" he exclaimed.

"Could it be a machine or a tool?" Mr. Banks wondered to himself.

A week later the ponko arrived. What do you think it was?

On a separate piece of paper, draw a picture of the ponko. Then describe it in detail and tell where the Banks family will put it.

A Nice Place for Mice

Your family of five white mice has been living in a cardboard box since you brought them home from the pet store two weeks ago. Now you feel it is time that they have a fancier, more permanent home.

Design a wonderful new home for your little friends in the space below. Draw a picture of their new habitat and label the various parts to show where your mice eat, play, sleep, and exercise.

Think Bigger!
© 1993—The Learning Works, Inc.

The Case of the Missing Giraffe

Detective: My name is Sergeant Sam Sunday, and I am here to investigate the robbery you reported at the Super Duper Toy Store. You say that a valuable toy giraffe disappeared from the store.

Manager: That's right, Sergeant Sunday. I was locking the doors at 9:00 p.m. when I noticed the giraffe had been taken. The only customers in the store before closing time were the members of the *Gee We Love Giraffes Club.*

Detective: The way I see it, whoever left the store last must have stolen the giraffe.

    Can you determine who stole the giraffe? On the next page are the times the club members left the store. Determine who was the last club member to leave. Then write the name of the giraffe thief below.

_____

Name _____

The *Gee We Love Giraffes* Club Members

Gloria Gould

35 minutes after
Glenda Green

Gilda Giles

25 minutes before
Guy Garber

George Gompers

An hour before store
closing time

Gordon Grimes

40 minutes after
Gilbert Gaines

Gaye Gaston

1 hour, 15 minutes
before Gus Givens

Guy Garber

5 minutes after
Gloria Gould

Glenda Green

15 minutes after
George Gompers

Gus Givens

15 minutes after
Gilda Giles

Gilbert Gaines

10 minutes after
Gaye Gaston

Think Bigger!
© 1993—The Learning Works, Inc.

Dream Team

Pretend you have been named captain of the Oakwood School baseball team. Choose a name for your team. In the space below, design a uniform using your team's colors, and draw a mascot for your team. On a separate piece of paper, write at least one of the following:

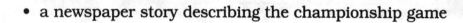

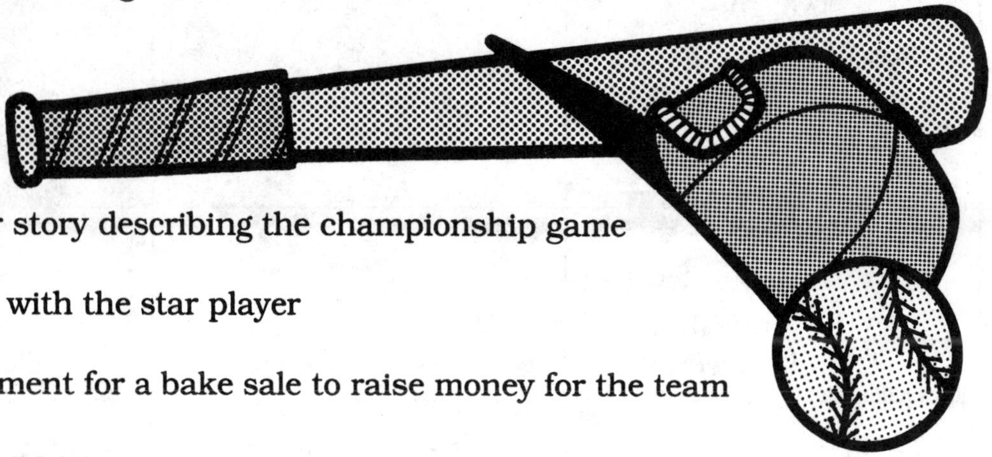

- a team song

- a cheer

- a newspaper story describing the championship game

- an interview with the star player

- an advertisement for a bake sale to raise money for the team

Team name: _____

Name _____

Pet Shells

Pretend you want to start a business called Pet Shells.

- What are Pet Shells?

- How much will each Pet Shell cost?

- Who will buy Pet Shells?

- Where will you advertise?

Plan your sales campaign. On a separate piece of paper, write and illustrate an ad for a magazine to convince people that they need Pet Shells. Write the directions that will be packaged with each Pet Shell. Tell how to care for it and make imaginative suggestions for its use.

Think Bigger!
© 1993—The Learning Works, Inc.

Rubber Band Bonanza

"I can't bear to part with them," Mrs. Baxter wept, as she gazed sadly at her gigantic collection—boxes piled to the top of her garage, filled with over 80,000,000 rubber bands. She had been saving rubber bands of all kinds, sizes, and colors since her son first started his paper route.

"I know I should get rid of them, but I want to put them to good use," Mrs. Baxter decided.

The following day Mrs. Baxter put this ad in the local paper:

> **FREE:** I will give my vast collection of rubber bands to the person who has the most creative uses for them. Come to 124 Maple Tree Lane on Saturday to submit your bid.

See if you can be the one to win Mrs. Baxter's rubber band collection. Work with a partner to make a list of at least ten creative ways to use Mrs. Baxter's rubber bands.

Ten uses for 80,000,000 rubber bands:

1. _____

2. _____

3. _____

4. _____

5. _____

6. _____

7. _____

8. _____

9. _____

10. _____

The Rock Band Van

The *Moonbeams*, a popular rock band, travel from city to city giving concerts for their thousands of enthusiastic fans. Since they are on the road for so long, they travel in a large van. The van pulls a trailer carrying the *Moonbeams'* instruments, costumes, and props.

Since the *Moonbeams* cook, sleep, read, play board games, watch television, and exercise in the van, it has to be a custom luxury vehicle, equipped with all kinds of features for their comfort and enjoyment.

On a separate piece of paper, draw a design of the inside of the *Moonbeams'* van. Write a paragraph describing the van in detail.

27

You are Invited

You have started your own after-school business creating custom party invitations on your personal computer. You have been promoting your business by circulating a flyer around town advertising your services. There has been a tremendous response to your advertisment, and orders are stacking up.

Here are some of the orders you have received for custom invitations:

- a birthday party for a lion cub at the zoo
- the grand opening of a magic store
- the skateboarding tournament at a local park
- the opening night of a new take-out restaurant
- a special showing of the works of the famous artist, Gabby the Gorilla

Choose one of these events and create an invitation for it on a separate piece of paper. Remember to include the following information in your invitation:

1. name of the host/hostess
2. the place
3. the date and time
4. any additional information, such as what guests should wear or bring
5. a telephone number to RSVP
6. a clever design on the front

Name _____

Pie Tin Creations

The Yummy Pies Restaurant serves delicious pies. The owners of Yummy Pies care about recycling and have asked all of their customers to bring in their aluminum pie tins. In return, they get a free piece of pie for every six tins they return.

They now have too many tins. Help the restaurant by designing a vehicle, creature, or sculpture using some of their extra pie tins. You may add other items to your creation. Draw and label your creation in the space below. If you have access to a number of pie tins, try to construct the creation you designed.

29

Think Bigger!
© 1993—The Learning Works, Inc.

Create a Cartoon

Create a new human or animal cartoon character with special powers. Draw a picture of your hero or heroine here and give him or her a name. My hero/heroine: _____

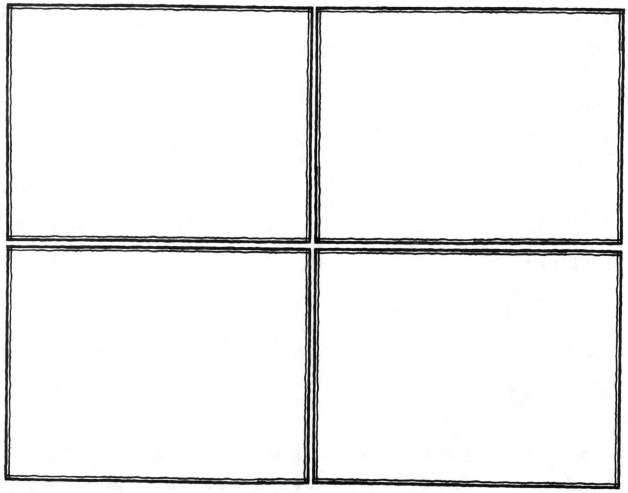

Draw a four-box comic strip featuring your character in the space below.

Invent a Word

Invent a new word. Look at the five groups of letters below.

1.	A	F	W	J	X	E
2.	E	B	V	N	R	U
3.	I	C	Z	P	O	Y
4.	O	G	K	M	D	A
5.	U	H	L	C	T	I

Use each letter group to invent a new word. Your word can name a person, animal, place, or thing. Letters in the group may be used in any order. You do not have to use all of the letters in the group, but your word must contain at least one vowel so that the word can be pronounced.

For each new word you invent, write a paragraph describing it. Then draw a picture of your creation.

Example:

E	N	L	S	Z	A

New word: "slenz"

A *slenz* looks a lot like a spider, but it has sixteen legs. Its head and body are gray, and it has black and white legs. The *slenz* can move very fast, but it cannot fly. It catches insects to eat and can spin its web in less than a minute.

Think Bigger!
© 1993—The Learning Works, Inc.

Name _____

The Magnificent Mercardo

"Ladies and gentlemen, watch as I transform this simple pumpkin into a work of art right before your eyes." Mercardo the magician deftly cut off the top of the pumpkin with one quick stroke. Then, taking an ice pick, he pricked six small holes in the bottom. His assistant poured planting mix in while Mercardo got three tiny geranium cuttings ready to place on top.

"Presto-change-o!" he exclaimed, as the pumpkin suddenly became a flower pot, bursting with colorful blooms.

Now it's your turn. Look at the list of objects on the next page. Choose one or two of them and think about what you could make out of each of these objects. Then, on a separate piece of paper, do the following:

- Explain what you can make from the object.

- Tell how you would take the object apart and reassemble it.

- Describe any parts that need to be added.

- Tell what it would be used for.

- Give it a name.

The Magnificent Mercardo
(continued)

surfboard	bedspread	wooden box
automobile tire	two skateboards	large backpack
six feathers	twenty-four small seashells	pencil sharpener
wagon	empty refrigerator carton	lamp shade

Think Bigger!
© 1993—The Learning Works, Inc.

Robots

Robots are mechanical devices that can be programmed to perform mental or physical tasks. They can be constructed in any shape or size suited to the work they must do.

For example, Mrs. Bishop, the manager of a paint store, needs to move heavy paint cans from the shelves in her stockroom to the delivery truck. Here is a description of her robot.

It looks a little like a small boxcar with big "arms." The "arms" telescope out to reach high places and to grasp paint cans from the top shelves. With the cans in its "hands," the robot rolls on its wheels to the rear of the delivery truck. It lowers the cans, releasing them onto the truck bed. It then pivots on its wheels and rolls back to the stockroom where it repeats the process.

On the next page is a list of some jobs that need to be done. Draw a picture of a robot that could do each job. On a separate piece of paper, write a paragraph in which you tell how one of the robots does its work.

Robots
(continued)

- Paula Windsor owns a pickle factory that produces hundreds of jars of pickles each day. As the filled jars roll past them on an assembly line, workers must place a lid on each pickle jar, closing it tightly. Design a robot that can put the lids on Paula's pickle jars.

- Roger Brown sells cartons of logs to people who have fireplaces in their homes. Each carton contains twenty logs. The logs are stacked in huge piles in Roger's lumberyard. Design a robot that can take logs from the pile, pack them in cartons, and staple the cartons shut.

- Eddie Jones likes to go fishing, but he would rather read a book beside the lake than hold his fishing rod. Design a robot that can catch fish for Eddie.

Think Bigger!
© 1993—The Learning Works, Inc.

Take Me Out to the Ball Game

"Come with me to a ball game," Angela's father announced on Monday evening. He smiled slyly as he added, "This game, however, is unlike any game you have ever seen before."

"What do you mean?" Angela asked. "Is it a baseball, basketball, or soccer game?"

"This new game is baseball, soccer, volleyball, and basketball, all combined into one exciting outdoor game," her father replied.

Pretend that you are at the ball game with Angela and her father. On a separate piece of paper, write a paragraph describing the game. Include the following in your description:

- the name of the game
- the object of the game
- the kind of ball used

- the number of teams and players
- what the players do with the ball
- how the players score points

In the space below, draw one or two of the players in action.

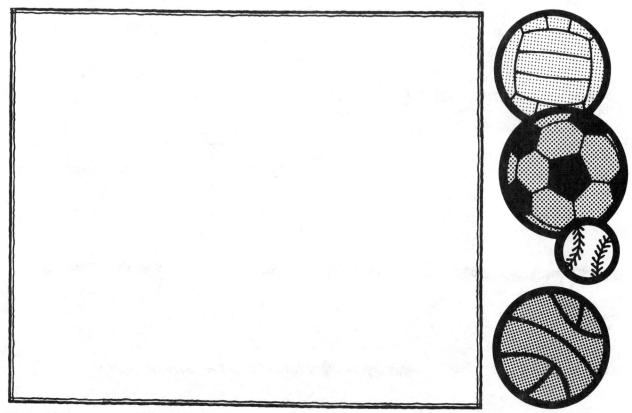

1-800 Numbers

Phone numbers can be hard to remember unless there is something unusual about them. Companies like to devise numbers that reflect the service they provide. For example, 1-800-738-2273 is hard to remember, but 1-800 PET CARE won't let you forget the number of Dr. Victoria, the veterinarian.

Here are some examples:

- Midville Diet Center   **1-800 GET THIN**

- Smith's Sporting Goods   **1-800 4 SPORTS**

- Myron's Barber Shop   **1-800 HAIRCUT**

- Shadyside Bookstore   **1-800 READ NOW**

Make up ten business names and create a toll-free telephone number for each. Write the names of the businesses on the left side of your paper and the telephone numbers on the right. Be sure to mix up the answers as you write them. Remember that a toll-free telephone number starts with 1-800 and ends with seven digits.

After you have finished, work with a partner and see if you can match each other's numbers and businesses.

37

The Strange Disappearance of Agatha Singleton

"Hello, Mary Ann? This is John Singleton. Have you seen Agatha? I'm a little uneasy. It's 6:00 and she was due home at 5:00."

"No, John, I haven't seen her since I met her earlier at Ralph's Sewing Center. She said she was hurrying to an appointment for her allergy shot. I hope she's O.K."

"I'll just approach this logically," John murmured, as he hung up the phone. "I'll just call each person on her *Things To Do* list beside the phone, and I'll be sure to locate her."

John Singleton was correct. He soon located Agatha. With a partner, discuss what each person on the next page told him, and see if you can figure out what happened to Agatha Singleton. Write a paragraph explaining your solution to the mystery.

The Strange Disappearance of Agatha Singleton
(continued)

Mrs. Kulpepper, counter person at Sue's Cleaners 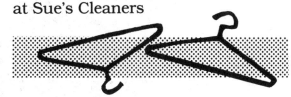	"I waited on Agatha at the dry cleaners. She said she was on her way to buy some geraniums and petunias for her garden."
Laura Frazier, friend 	"I met Mrs. Singleton for tea and cake at the English Garden Restaurant. She told me she was going to look at some papers in her safe deposit box, but had to hurry as they lock the bank vault at 4:30."
Rex Roberts, Roberts' Repair Shop 	"I waited on her in my store. She mentioned that she was on her way to buy some fabric to make a pair of pants for her nephew."
Miss Birch, next door neighbor 	"I visited with Agatha when she dropped off my order of Girl Scout cookies. She said she was taking her winter coat to the dry cleaners.
Sam Winters, manager of Glorious Gardens 	"I talked with her at the nursery. She said she was in a hurry to pick up her toaster from the repair shop before it closed."
Dr. Yates, Young Medical Clinic 	"I overheard her telling my nurse that she was looking forward to a nice cup of tea and a piece of cake."

Think Bigger!
© 1993—The Learning Works, Inc.

Bing Bong

King Kong, ping pong, ding dong—put them all together and you get BING BONG! No, it's not a humongous gorilla playing table tennis. It's a game waiting to be invented—by YOU.

What You Need:

- scratch paper (for rough draft)
- white posterboard for final playing board
- encyclopedias and reference materials for research
- felt-tipped markers, pencils
- rulers
- scissors
- colored art paper for question cards (2" x 4")
- glue (for attaching rules to the inside of the box cover)
- dice or spinner
- tokens for up to four players
- a box large enough to hold all game contents except the playing board

Contents of Game:

- dice or spinner
- playing pieces for two to four players
- question cards
- chance cards
- answer booklet
- rules and directions for play
- playing board

Bing Bong
(continued)

What You Do:

1. Design a rough draft of your game board. Make sure the name of your game, Bing Bong, is clear and easy to read on the board.

2. Make up about thirty question cards using reference books. Also add some chance cards to make your game interesting.

3. Copy the rough draft of your game board design on white posterboard. Use a ruler and work neatly. Add pictures to make your board attractive and fun. Color your board.

4. Make or collect four different game tokens. You may use bottle caps, coins, spools, shells, or other items.

5. Cover a box with paper for your game contents such as dice, question and chance cards, play money, spinners, etc. (Your board does not have to fit inside the box.)

6. Paste your rules and directions inside the box cover. Your rules should answer the following questions:

   a. What is the object of the game?

   b. Who goes first?

   c. What do you do when you land on a space?

   d. Who checks the answers in the answer booklet?

   e. What happens if you answer a question correctly? Incorrectly?

   f. When is the game over?

7. You can use the name Bing Bong in other creative ways. It can be words players call out if they land on a specific place on your board. Bing Bong can be a location on your game board or something a player does, such as moving ahead three spaces.

Think Bigger!
© 1993—The Learning Works, Inc.

Name ______________________

Worlds of Wonder

Worlds of Wonder, an amusement park that will open next year, has asked you to design an exciting new ride. Complete the following:

Name of the ride: ______________________

What is the theme of the ride? ______________________

____

____

____

Do the riders stand or sit? ______________________

What kind of seatbelt or other restraining device will be used to keep riders safe?

____

____

Describe the lighting on your ride: ______________________

____

____

Describe the sounds the riders hear: ______________________

____

____

____

Are there any other special effects used? ______________________

____

____

____

The ride is appropriate for:

children under 6   ages 6–12   teenagers   adults

(Circle all that apply)

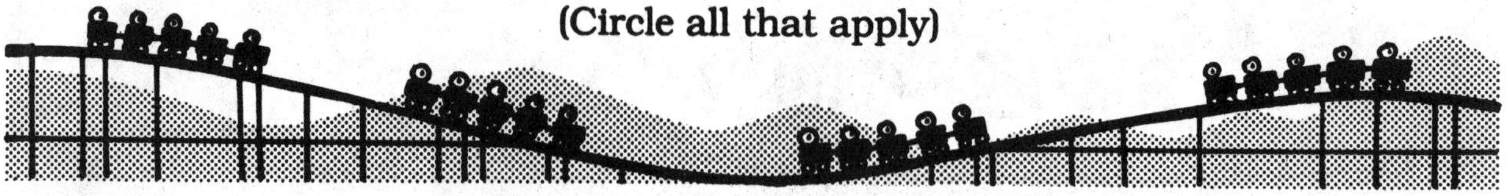

© 1993—The Learning Works, Inc.

Worlds of Wonder
(continued)

In the space below, draw your new ride.

Think Bigger!
© 1993—The Learning Works, Inc.

The Go-Go Cart Company

Besides making carts for golfers, the Go-Go Cart Company designs and builds *special* carts for people who need them for their work. For example, they made a special cart for the equipment manager of the Tigers Baseball Team. They painted the Tigers' name and logo on the side of a bright orange cart. In the back of the cart they made compartments for baseball bats. They attached two little wagons to the cart for carrying gloves, bases, balls, and the catcher's equipment.

Imagine that you are the designer for the Go-Go Cart Company. On a separate piece of paper, create a special cart for one of the people listed below. Sketch and color the cart you design. Label the parts to show how they work.

- a circus clown
- a forest ranger
- the gardener for a public park
- a carpenter
- a house painter
- a zookeeper

Name _____

Holiday Happenings

Create a new holiday. Your holiday can be based on an important event in history, a myth, or a special person's birthday. On a separate piece of paper, complete the following:

- Select a date for your holiday.

- State the reason for this special occasion.

- Design a greeting card people can send on your holiday.

- Write a short paragraph describing ways people celebrate this holiday. Include special foods that are eaten and games that are played.

Think Bigger!
© 1993—The Learning Works, Inc.

Ice Cream Heaven

Pretend you are opening a unique ice cream parlor called Ice Cream Heaven. Your store sells flavors such as *Chips, Chunks, Chimps 'n Chocolate*. This chocolate ice cream contains caramel chips, chunks of toffee, and chocolate candies shaped like chimpanzees. The menu describes it as:

> a crunchy, no monkey business combo
> of chocolate ice cream loaded with
> chocolate chimps, caramel, and toffee.

On the following page, create a menu with six new ice cream flavors. Include their names, ingredients, and mouth-watering descriptions. Illustrate your menu.

Ice Cream Heaven
(continued)

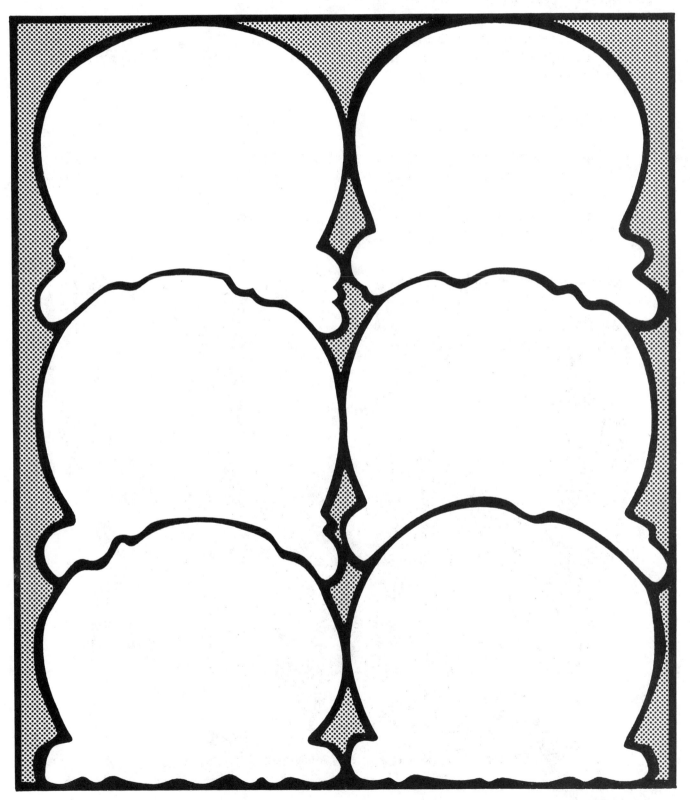

Think Bigger!
© 1993—The Learning Works, Inc.

Wild West Tours

As a successful tour director for Wild West Tours, you take clients on trips to the western part of the United States.

Choose one of the new clients on the next page and plan an itinerary that will match the client's interests and hobbies. Then do the following on a separate piece of paper:

- List the names and locations of the places to visit.

- Write a paragraph including basic information such as climate, clothing needed, and things to see and do.

- Write a paragraph in which you describe the adventurous routes Wild West Tours will take to the various places.

Wild West Tours
(continued)

Harvey Hammer

"I am a sailor, surfer, water-skier, and scuba diver. I'm looking for some new places to enjoy water sports."

Dr. Newmarker

"I love to visit the sites of historical events so that I can view relics of the past."

Sarah Bates-Talbot

"I am a bird watcher, and I like to visit places where I am likely to see birds."

Carl Banner

"My hobby is eating, and I love food from all countries. I enjoy talking with chefs and sharing recipes."

Marian Hill

"As an artist, I paint landscapes—wide-open spaces. I love to visit places where there are not many people or buildings."

Paula Ortega

"As a geologist, I want to examine specimens from the earth's past. I want to visit a place where I can explore caves and unique rock formations."

Think Bigger!
© 1993—The Learning Works, Inc.

Fun with Commercials

Pretend you are on the staff of the Zing Advertising Corporation. Your job is to write a brief script that will amuse television viewers and prompt them to buy the advertised product.

Choose one of the following products. On a separate piece of paper, write a commercial for the product. You may use illustrations to make it more interesting. Your commercial should not last more than one minute. Read the sample script on the following page for ideas.

The Porcupine, a small truck	*Gooey Chewy,* bubble gum	*Enerjuice,* a health drink
O'Hara, a personal computer	*Bug Battle,* an electronic game	*Flight,* sports shoes

Fun with Commercials
(continued)

Hash for Hounds
A Television Commercial

Scene: A man and woman each walking their dogs on tree-lined street. The woman's dog is big, frisky, healthy looking. The man's dog is thin, droopy, tired.

SUE

Ed, what's the matter with Rusty? He's so thin, and he has no pep.

ED

Rusty won't eat the dog food I give him. I've tried all the brands in the supermarket, and he doesn't like any of them. I don't know what to do.

SUE

I feed my Fritzy *Hash For Hounds*. It comes in three flavors—beef, chicken, and liver. Fritzy loves them all.

ED

But is *Hash For Hounds* good for dogs?

SUE

Yes, it's filled with vitamins and minerals. It's low in fat, and it has no sugar, salt, or preservatives. It tastes good—and it's not expensive.

ED

Thanks for the advice. I'll get *Hash For Hounds* for Rusty today.

Scene: Same place, one week later. Ed riding bike, dog running beside him, fit and healthy. They meet Sue with Fritzy.

SUE

Ed, you and Rusty look terrific! What's happened since I saw you last week?

ED

It's *Hash For Hounds*—Rusty liked it so much that I decided to try it too. Now we both feel great!

Think Bigger!
© 1993—The Learning Works, Inc.

On the Other Side of the Jungle

"Come quickly, Dr. Anderson! We have found it at last—the magnificent land on the other side of the rain forest. Follow me. The jungle ends five hundred feet from here, and there you will see it—surrounded on two sides by jungle, on one side by rolling hills, and on the other by the ocean."

Dr. Anderson turned to the weary group of scientists who had been exploring with him. "Hurry, everyone! We are about to reach our goal, the beautiful, uninhabited land the natives told us about. I was beginning to think that it was only a myth, but it lies just ahead."

You are with the group of scientists. The group decides that the land is the perfect place for them to settle permanently in order to continue their research. They form teams to make plans for the community.

Work with a partner to complete the tasks listed on the next page.

On the Other Side of the Jungle
(continued)

- Make a map of the land. Show features such as mountains, hills, valleys, deserts, lakes, rivers, fields, and forests.

- Make a list of the land's natural resources—plants, animals, fish, rivers, lakes, timber, rocks, and minerals.

- List ways in which you can use the land's rich resources while causing as little damage as possible to the environment.

- Write a paragraph explaining what supplies you will need from the outside world. Tell how you will import these supplies.

Think Bigger!
© 1993—The Learning Works, Inc.

Recycled Junk Sculptures

Turn recycled junk into a work of art.

Do the following:

- Collect an assortment of reusable items, such as boxes, bags, cans, paper cups, junk mail, spools, and straws.

- Make a sculpture out of the reusable materials. Use tape, glue, and/or staples to hold your sculpture together.

- Decorate your sculpture with colored paper, marking pens, or paint.

- Mount your sculpture on a cardboard base and give it a title. Exhibit your art for others to enjoy.

Sand Sculptures

The annual Sand Sculpture Festival at Sea Cliff Beach attracts people from miles around. They build sand sculptures of people, animals, cartoon characters, buildings, and miniature cities to compete for prizes.

Plan a sand sculpture that you can enter in the Sea Cliff contest. Draw a sketch of your creation below. Try to actually build your sculpture using sand or modeling clay.

55

Think Bigger!
© 1993—The Learning Works, Inc.

Campaign Time

Pretend you are running for the office of president of the student council at your school. On a separate piece of paper, write a plan for your campaign and create a slogan. Design posters, signs, campaign buttons, bumper stickers for bicycles, or other things you think will help your classmates become more familiar with your name. Write a short speech to give at a school assembly prior to election day. Tell why students should elect you president.

Name _____

Create a Collection

Imagine you own a company that makes unusual sports cards similar in size and shape to the baseball and football cards on the market.

Make ten sports cards for your company, using 3"x5" index cards. Draw pictures on the front of the card and write descriptions for ten unusual sports on the backs of the cards. To make the cards unique, invent your own sports, teams, and players to feature on the cards.

Think Bigger!
© 1993—The Learning Works, Inc.

Miranda Cooper's Amazing Copy Machine

When Mr. Fieldstone retired and gave up his business, he sold everything in his office—desks, chairs, typewriters, and a small copy machine. "Everything goes!" he said happily, as he directed the movers.

Miranda Cooper, a woman with a small home office, bought the copy machine. She set it up in her tiny, cluttered office, then locked the door and finished preparing for a trip she had been planning for a long time. The next day she left on a year-long cruise around the world.

Soon after she returned from her trip, Miranda decided that it was time to get to work again. "I have to tidy up that office and get on with the business," she murmured as she unlocked her office door. "Oh, there's that copy machine I bought just before I left," she said. "I wonder if it works."

She loaded the paper tray, turned the machine on, placed a letter on it, and pressed the START button. The machine hummed, and out came a crisp copy of her letter. But the machine kept on humming, and out came a second paper with a picture of a coupon on it. On the coupon were the words: "Redeemable for $1,000 at your local bank." At the bottom of the page were the words: "P.S. Run, do not walk, to your nearest bank. This coupon expires at midnight tonight."

"This is impossible, but I'm not taking any chances," Miranda said as she put the coupon into her purse and hurried to her bank. Feeling a little embarrassed, she handed the coupon to the teller. "I hope they don't think I'm holding up the bank," she thought, glancing nervously at the security monitors in the ceiling.

Without hesitation, the teller handed Miranda ten $100 bills. Miranda tried to look calm as she tucked them into her handbag and thanked the teller.

Miranda Cooper's Amazing Copy Machine
(continued)

Miranda was somewhat curious as she approached her copy machine the next day, but she had work to do. By now she was wondering if she had discovered a modern-day Aladdin's magic lamp! "I can't believe this luck," Miranda said to herself, "I had better unplug this machine for awhile and give it a little rest, or it might change its way of doing things."

The next day Miranda shakily plugged the machine in again. She made a copy of her telephone bill. Then a second sheet of paper came out, but in place of a coupon, a heavy black outline framed the words: "Your dog has chewed up all of your neighbor's rose bushes. Pay your neighbor $200 at once."

Miranda ran to the window in a panic, and there was her dog, romping joyously through the neighbor's flower garden. "Oh, dear," she moaned, "what made the machine change its mind?"

In the following week Miranda continued to use her amazing copy machine. Each time the copier produced a copy of the original, plus one other piece of paper with a message, until there were seven messages in all—some good news, some bad news.

Using your imagination, write the seven messages that came out of Miranda Cooper's amazing copy machine. Then choose your favorite message and describe in detail what Miranda said and did after she received the message.

59

Think Bigger!
© 1993—The Learning Works, Inc.

Mark Matson, the Motorcycle-Maker

Mark Matson designs and builds motorcycles used for transportation, pleasure, and sports. He specializes in customized vehicles of all sizes, many with special features such as windshields, passenger seats, sidecars, or saddlebags. Engine and tire size are also tailored to the customer's taste.

Read about some of Mark's customers on the following page. Choose one, and design a motorcycle for this client. On a separate piece of paper, make a drawing of the motorcycle. Label the parts and custom features. Then write a short article for *Motorcyclist* magazine, describing the motorcycle and its special features.

Below are some of the features you might want to include:

- engine
- wheels
- rider's seat
- handlebars
- two rear-view mirrors

- brakes
- headlight and rear light
- fuel gauge
- rider's foot rest
- exhaust pipe

Mark Matson, the Motorcycle-Maker
(continued)

Nick Green

"I deliver packages for Whizzing Wheels Delivery Service. I need a motorcycle to navigate narrow city streets in heavy traffic."

Michelle Sanders

"I'm eight years old, and I compete in junior motocross events. I race on cross-country courses over rough, muddy ground."

Arthur Browne

"I want to take my dog Bernie, a Saint Bernard, with me on my vacations."

Clint Jones

"As a successful movie actor, I'm looking for a flashy vehicle to drive around town. I'm willing to pay for luxury and custom features."

Think Bigger!
© 1993—The Learning Works, Inc.

Whatever Became of Peter Pratt?

"We'll always be friends," laughed nine-year-old Jeremy Hatfield, as he, Peter, and Susan looked happily at the fort they had just built together.

Ten years later, Jeremy Hatfield and Susan Yates met for lunch in the college cafeteria at Arizona State University. "Whatever became of Peter Pratt?" Jeremy asked as they carried their pizza to the table. "After his family moved when we were in sixth grade, I heard from him once, then never again."

"I lost track of him, too. Then suddenly one day I saw his name in the paper. He's led an amazing life filled with adventure, travel, and danger. I even started keeping a scrapbook of clippings about his exploits. I'll show it to you next time we get together," she promised.

When Susan brought the scrapbook a week later, Jeremy saw dozens of headlines like these:

Peter Pratt Captures Rare Parrot in Amazon Basin

Pratt Solves Baffling Case of Missing Star

On a separate piece of paper, write ten more imaginative headlines for news stories on Peter Pratt's adventures. Choose your favorite headline and write a one-page feature article for it. Give details about the adventure, and include a quotation by Peter. Illustrate the article.

A Letter to Chelsea

In January 1993, a twelve-year-old girl, Chelsea Clinton, went to live at the White House in Washington, D.C. when her father became president of the United States.

Pretend that you are the son or daughter of a past president. Write a letter to Chelsea Clinton telling her about the interesting experiences you had when you lived in the White House. Describe famous people you met and special occasions you celebrated in the White House. Tell what it was like as the son or daughter of a president. Give Chelsea some advice based on your experiences. Before you begin, do research on the president you select so that your letter is based on actual events that occurred during the president's term of office.

Think Bigger!
© 1993—The Learning Works, Inc.

Plan a Town

Congratulations! You are the newly appointed president of New Century Towns, a development company with creative ideas.

Your company has bought a tract of land from Shadyside Development, a company that has recently gone bankrupt. Shadyside had begun to develop the land by building all the streets first. Their unfinished town looks like the drawing on the next page.

Give your town a name and finish designing it. Think about the places and services that a town needs, and include them on the map. Make your town a place where people will enjoy living.

Write an ad for the real estate section of your newspaper. Describe your town's best features so that people will want to live and work in your community.

Plan a Town
(continued)

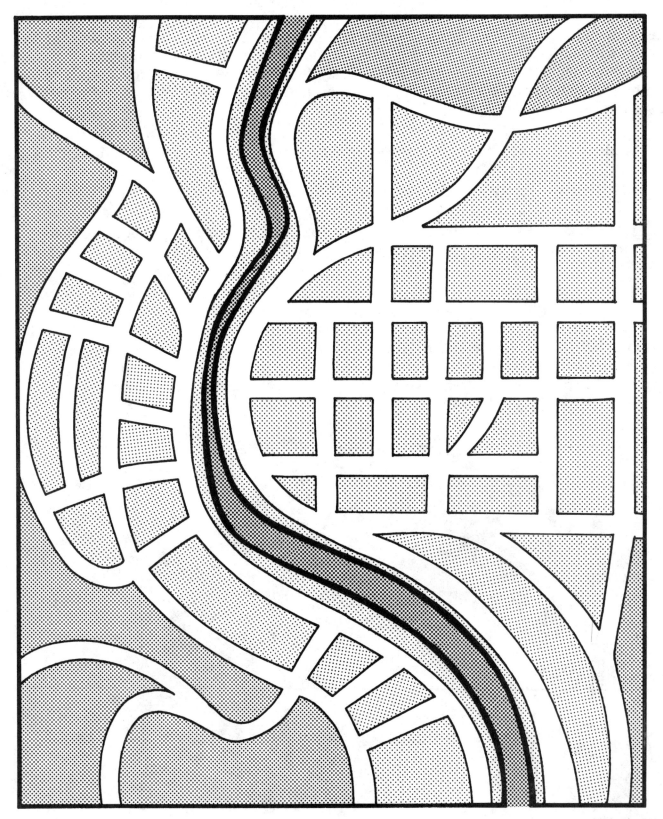

Think Bigger!
© 1993—The Learning Works, Inc.

Life on the Moon

Have you ever looked at the sky on a clear night and wondered what it would be like to visit the moon? Although scientists have studied the moon with telescopes for hundreds of years, man's first exploration of the moon did not take place until July 20, 1969, when two American astronauts, Neil Armstrong and Edwin Aldrin, Jr., landed on the moon. They took hundreds of photographs and collected specimens of moon rocks and soil. Over the next few years, other astronauts explored the surface of the moon.

Studies and explorations of the moon have revealed a number of interesting facts:

• There is no air, water, or sound on the moon.

• The moon's terrain is made up of huge boulders, dust-covered plains, jagged mountains, and deep craters.

• The force of gravity on the moon is so weak that someone who can jump four feet high on earth could jump twenty-four feet high on the moon.

Pretend it is the year 2178. You and your family live on the moon. On a separate piece of paper, write a letter to a friend back on Earth. Explain how you survive on the moon. Tell what your life is like, and describe your home, school, and community. Explain what you do for recreation.

Four Friendly Frogs

An **alliteration** is a group of words that begin with the same sound, such as Peter Piper picked a peck of pickled peppers.

Write and illustrate a book of alliterations. To make your book, you will need a front and back cover, plus thirteen pages. Use one side of each page to write an alliteration using each letter of the alphabet. Also make the title of your book an alliteration.

Think Bigger!
© 1993—The Learning Works, Inc.

Ix Initials

Pretend you find yourself in the faraway fantasy land of Ix. Looking about, you see that you are in a town with peculiar signs—*G.S.*, *D.N.E.*, and *R.G.A.P.*

"They are using initials instead of words," you say to yourself. "*G.S.* has to mean *Gas Station*, and that is surely a *Do Not Enter* sign. But what can *R.G.A.P.* mean?"

A passerby hears your question and says, "Obviously, it is *Really Great Amusement Park.*"

Here are some more signs to figure out. On a separate piece of paper, write what you think they mean. When you finish, work with a partner to make ten more signs for Ix. Try to translate each other's signs.

B.R.	O.W.T.	D.I.	O.B.R.
P.S.	M.U.V.	F.Q.T.	M.I.
N.Z.A.	H.	S.E.	U.F.F.
Q.Z.	C.E.G.	L.P.	V.I.D.P.

Name _____

Mixed-Up Animals

You have been asked to design a new animal for Fun For All, a company that makes stuffed animals. Combine different parts from as many animals as you can to create a humorous creature you think kids will enjoy. Draw and color your stuffed animal on a separate sheet of paper. Make a name tag to attach to it.

Your class can divide into groups to make the animals as a fun project. Here's how:

- Form groups of five or six students. Each group draws and colors a complete stuffed animal, then cuts apart the head, body, tail, etc.

- The teacher collects the heads, shuffles them, and passes different heads back to the groups.

- Repeat the process for the tails, bodies, feet, etc., until each group has parts for a funny new animal.

- Paste the mixed-up animal onto a sheet of white art paper. Add other features. Give it a name tag and write a short description of it.

- Display the animals your class has created as a Mixed-Up Animal Zoo.

Think Bigger!
© 1993—The Learning Works, Inc.

Rachel's Route

After picking up her newspapers early each morning from the *Zimba News Company*, Rachel Richards will deliver them in the village of Lugano. She wants to plan her route carefully to save time.

Listed below are the twelve places on Rachel's route.

Rachel's Delivery List

A. Acme Drug Store

B. Bob's Newsstand

C. Central Plaza Hotel

D. Dayton's Restaurant

E. Ethel's Coffee Shop

F. Frank's Diner

G. Grace's Gifts and News

H. Healthy Valley Hospital

I. Inn at South Park

J. Jack's Sports Club

K. Kate's Cookie Kitchen

L. Lugano Bus Station

- Study the map on the next page so that you can draw a timesaving route for Rachel. Start at **Z**, *Zimba News Company*. Then go to all twelve places, finally returning to **Z**.

- After you have drawn the route, write a delivery list. Show the places in the order in which Rachel will deliver her newspapers.

Name _____

Rachel's Route

(continued)

The Village of Lugano

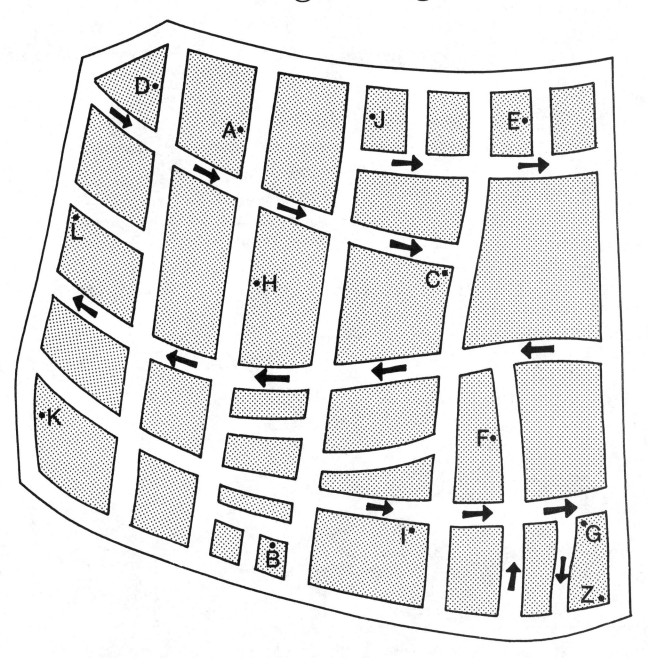

The capital letters mark the stops on Rachel's route. She begins and ends at **Z**, the *Zimba News Company*. In planning a timesaving route, watch out for dead-end and one-way streets. The arrows on the map show the direction of the one-way streets.

Think Bigger!
© 1993—The Learning Works, Inc.

Name _____

Cloud Creations

On a cloudy day make pencil sketches of some unusual shapes of clouds. After you have outlined them on paper, look carefully at the cloud shapes you have made. Use your imagination to think of things they resemble. With your pencil, add details to the cloud shapes to create the things you have imagined. Here is an example:

After you finish your cloud drawing, write a one-page story based on the picture you have drawn.

Bike of the Future

Design a bike of the future. How will it be different from the bikes of today? Draw your bike in the space below. Label its special features and explain how they work.

MIRROR

LIE BACK, GO BACKWARDS ON A BACKABIKE

Think Bigger!
© 1993—The Learning Works, Inc.

Compound Capers

The words *hilltop*, *football*, and *doorbell* are all compound words. Compound words are words made up of two smaller words. Play a word game by creating humorous new compound words. Start by taking two compounds and dividing them into two smaller words. For example:

camp	*fire*
gold	*fish*

Then, mix and match the word parts in different ways. For example, from the words above, you can make

campfish   and   *goldfire*

or you can have

campgold   and   *firefish.*

Another way to make comical compound words is to join any two words to create a new word. For example, if you combine *bug* and *bath,* you can make the new word *bugbath.* Draw pictures to go with the new words you create. For example:

Have more fun with your comical compounds by using them in poems, stories, or cartoons. On the line below, write a comical compound name for a cartoon character.

_____

Flags at the Fair

A brand new country, Flavia, wants you to design flags for the upcoming national fair in the country's capital. You are to design one flag for the country itself, and one flag for each of its two states. Be creative. The flags will fly proudly at the entrance to the fair. Design the three different flags below.

Think Bigger!
© 1993—The Learning Works, Inc.

Over the Rainbow

A violent tornado carries Dorothy and her dog, Toto, from their home in Kansas to a faraway land called Oz. Sound familiar? Pretend that, like Frank Baum, the author of *The Wizard of Oz*, you know a fantasy place "somewhere over the rainbow." You and your dog or other pet are whirled away to your imaginary land.

On a separate piece of paper:

• Describe the imaginary place and the creatures who live there.

• Tell about three adventures you and your pet have there.

• On the back of the paper, draw and color a map of the land. Label the places on the map where your adventures took place.

Answer Key

Page 9, Lost and Found

Karen found her lamb in the laundry basket. The lamb was moved about in the following order:

Person	From	To
Kurt	backyard	Ken's bedroom
Krista	Ken's bedroom	Ken's backpack
Ken	Ken's backpack	top of dishwasher
Kelly	dishwasher	under dining room table
Karl	dining room table	outside Kap's doghouse
Kerry	outside Kap's doghouse	behind sofa
Kyle	behind sofa	bookcase
Kim	bookcase	laundry basket

Page 12, Secret Codes

The patterns of shapes and dots for the consonants are:

tall consonants	circles with different numbers of dots
short consonants	different numbers of dots alone
consonants that go below the line	triangles with different numbers of dots

Max's message to Andy is "Meet me at the park at four."

Pages 22–23, The Case of the Missing Giraffe

The last person to leave the store was Guy Garber at 8:55. The departure times for each person are:

Gaye Gaston	7:30
Gilbert Gaines	7:40
George Gompers	8:00
Glenda Green	8:15
Gordon Grimes	8:20
Gilda Giles	8:30
Gus Givens	8:45
Gloria Gould	8:50
Guy Garber	8:55

Pages 38-39, The Strange Disappearance of Agatha Singleton

Here is the order of Agatha's activities and the people she saw:

1. Drop off cookies (Miss Birch)
2. Dry cleaners (Mrs. Kulpepper)
3. Gardening Center (Sam Winters)
4. Repair Shop (Rex Roberts)
5. Buy fabric (Mary Ann)
6. Get allergy shot (Dr. Yates)
7. Have tea and cake (Laura Frazier)
8. Go to the bank — Perhaps she accidentally got locked in the vault!

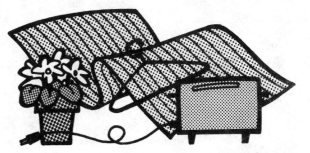

Think Bigger!
© 1993—The Learning Works, Inc.

Answer Key
(continued)

Pages 70–71, Rachel's Route

Rachel's Delivery List, in order:

1.	**F**	Frank's Diner
2.	**C**	Central Plaza Hotel
3.	**E**	Ethel's Coffee Shop
4.	**J**	Jack's Sports Club
5.	**H**	Healthy Valley Hospital
6.	**A**	Acme Drug Store
7.	**D**	Dayton's Restaurant
8.	**L**	Lugano Bus Station
9.	**K**	Kate's Cookie Kitchen
10.	**B**	Bob's Newsstand
11.	**I**	Inn at South Park
12.	**G**	Grace's Gifts and News

NOTES

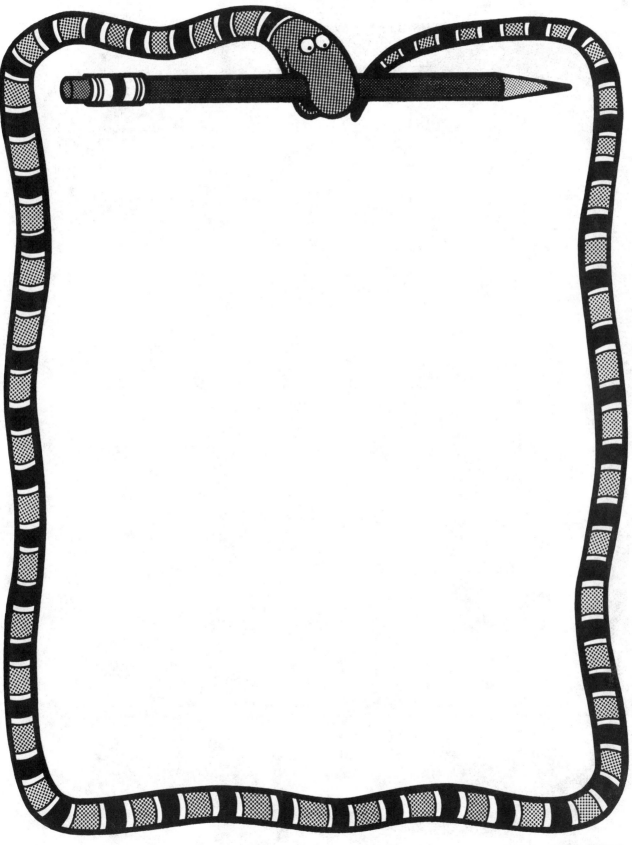

Think Bigger!
© 1993—The Learning Works, Inc.

NOTES

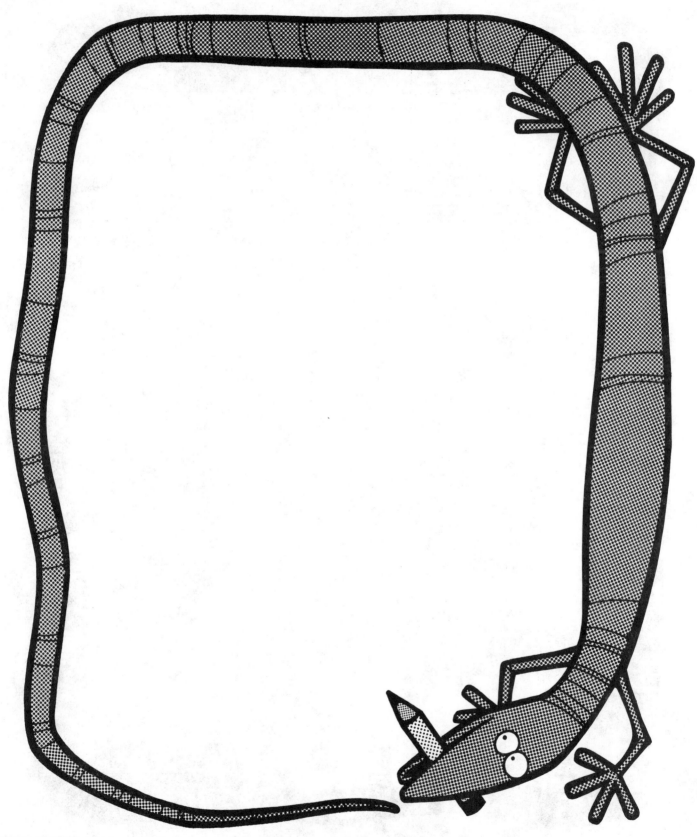